BIBLE NEWS PROPHECY

 19
 23
 32

In This Issue:

2   **From the Editor: God Says Prophecy is Important**.

4   **19 Prophetic Items to Watch For in 2019** Many events will align with properly understood biblical prophecies in 2019.

19   **The Second Commandment** Should you pay any attention to it?

23   **Study the Bible Course Lesson 14c What is Man?** What are humans anyway? Are humans immortal or can they be granted immortality?

32   **Youth and Singles Q&A** This article answers questions some teens and singles have wondered about.

Back Cover: Internet and Radio This shows where people can find the messages from the Continuing Church of God.

About the Front Cover: James Erwin Estoque put this together using Pixabay.com and Pexels.com available images.

Bible News Prophecy magazine is published by the Continuing Church of God, 1036 W. Grand Avenue, Grover Beach, CA, 93433. http://www.ccog.org

©2018 Continuing Church of God. Printed in the U.S.A. All rights reserved.

Reproduction in whole or in part without written permission is prohibited. We do respect your privacy and we do not rent, trade, or sell our mailing list. If you do not want to receive this magazine, simply contact our Grover Beach office. Scripture references are from the New King James Version (©Thomas Nelson, Inc., Publishers, used by permission or for 20th century articles the KJV) unless otherwise noted.

Bible News Prophecy-SUPPORTED BY YOUR CONTRIBUTIONS

Bible News Prophecy has no subscription or newsstand price. This magazine is provided free of charge by the Continuing Church of God. It is made possible by the voluntary, freely given tithes and offerings of the membership of the Church and others who have elected to support the work of the Church. Contributions are gratefully welcomed and are tax-deductible in the U.S. Those who wish to voluntarily aid and support this worldwide Work of God are gladly welcomed as co-workers in this major effort to preach and publish the gospel to all nations. Contributions should be sent to: Continuing Church of God, 1036 W. Grand Avenue, Grover Beach, CA, 93433.

Editor in Chief: Bob Thiel

Copy/Proofing Editor: Joyce Thiel

Proofreader: John Hickey; **SBC Course Assister:** Shirley Gestro.

Photos: All photos come from the Thiel family or public domain sources such as Wikipedia, Pixabay, or certain governments (unless specific attribution is given).

Layout and Design: James Erwin EStoque

January - March 2019

FROM THE EDITOR IN CHIEF: BOB THIEL

GOD SAYS PROPHECY IS IMPORTANT

Are properly understood biblical prophecies coming to pass?

Can you rely on Bible prophecy?

Well, God is clear that He makes prophetic statements and causes them to be fulfilled:

> 9 Remember the former things of old, For I am God, and there is no other; I am God, and there is none like Me,
> 10 Declaring the end from the beginning, And from ancient times things that are not yet done, Saying, 'My counsel shall stand, And I will do all My pleasure,'
> 11 Calling a bird of prey from the east, The man who executes My counsel, from a far country. Indeed I have spoken it; I will also bring it to pass. I have purposed it; I will also do it. (Isaiah 46:9-11, NKJV throughout, unless otherwise specified)

Fulfilled prophecy is part of the proof that God exists and should be real to your life EVERYDAY!

Between 1/5th and 1/3rd of the Bible is considered to be prophetic.

Since, "It is written, 'Man shall not live by bread alone, but by every word of God'" (Luke 4:4), knowing the prophetic word is important. All scripture, including prophecy, is important:

> 16 All Scripture is given by inspiration of God, and is profitable for doctrine, for reproof, for correction, for instruction in righteousness, 17 that the man of God may be complete, thoroughly equipped for every good work. (2 Timothy 3:16-17)

If you do not understand relevant prophecy, you will not "be complete, thoroughly equipped for every good work."

Notice something else from the New Testament:

> 9 Then he said to me, "Write: 'Blessed are those who are called to the marriage supper of the Lamb!'" And he said to me, "These are the true sayings of God." 10 And I fell at his feet to worship him. But he said to me, "See that you do not do that! I am your fellow servant, and of your brethren who have the testimony of Jesus. Worship God! For the testimony of Jesus is the spirit of prophecy." (Revelation 19:9-10)

Jesus fulfilled over 200 Old Testament prophecies (see our free book, Proof Jesus was the Messiah, available at www.ccog.org) and will fulfil more in the future.

Some, despite claiming to believe the Bible, either discount or overlook prophecy. But that is not supposed to be the case for true Christians:

> 29 "Look at the fig tree, and all the trees. 30 When they are already budding, you see and know for yourselves that summer is now near. 31 So you also, when you see these things happening, know that the kingdom of God is near. 32 Assuredly, I say to you, this generation will by no means pass away till all things take place. 33 Heaven and earth will pass away, but My words will by no means pass away.
>
> 34 "But take heed to yourselves, lest your hearts be weighed down with carousing, drunkenness, and cares of this life, and that Day come on you unexpectedly. 35 For it will come as a snare on all those who dwell on the face of the whole earth. 36 Watch therefore, and pray always that you may be counted worthy to escape all these things that will come to pass, and to stand before the Son of Man." (Luke 21:29-36)

Notice that Jesus taught that His followers will always have to pay attention to events and prophecies related to His return. Jesus repeatedly told His followers to watch for world events that would fulfill prophecy in other scriptures such as Matthew 24:42, 25:13; Mark 13:9,33,34,35,37, and Revelation 3:3. Jesus did expect His followers to watch.

By watching and praying to be accounted worthy, Christians are to be motivated to change.

However, scripture is clear that not all real Christians will be protected from what will come (Revelation 12:17), thus those who will not pay proper attention to prophecy will not realise what is happening until it is too late.

Jesus used prophecy to keep His followers vigilant—He wanted them to be 'hot' and not lukewarm (Revelation 3:14-22).

Jesus also taught that the Holy Spirit, "the Spirit of truth," would assist the faithful in understanding all truth, including prophetic ones:

> 12 I still have many things to say to you, but you cannot bear them now. 13 However, when ...the Spirit of truth, has come, {it} will guide you into all truth; ...will tell you things to come. (John 16:12-13)

Having the Holy Spirit and properly being led by the Holy Spirit helps us understand prophecy.

The Bible also teaches:

> 19 Do not quench the Spirit. 20 Do not despise prophecies. (1 Thessalonians 5:19-20)

Yet many do not seem to believe that God's Spirit is currently working prophetically now. Many also tend to despise biblical prophecies as well as, often, their proper explanation(s).

While some discount the importance of prophecy, notice what the Apostle Paul taught:

> 11 And do this, knowing the time, that now it is high time to awake out of sleep; for now our salvation is nearer than when we first believed. 12 The night is far spent, the day is at hand. Therefore let us cast off the works of darkness, and let us put on the armor of light. 13 Let us walk properly, as in the day, not in revelry and drunkenness, not in lewdness and lust, not in strife and envy. 14 But put on the Lord Jesus Christ, and make no provision for the flesh, to fulfill its lusts. (Romans 13:11-14)

Are we not a lot closer to the end now than when Paul wrote that? Paul also taught that true Christians were not to be like others who would not know near when Jesus would return (1 Thessalonians 5:4).

> 32 "But of that day and hour no one knows, not even the angels in heaven, nor the Son, but only the Father. 33 Take heed, watch and pray; for you do not know when the time is. 34 It is like a man going to a far country, who left his house and gave authority to his servants, and to each his work, and commanded the doorkeeper to watch. 35 Watch therefore, for you do not know when the master of the house is coming--in the evening, at midnight, at the crowing of the rooster, or in the morning-- 36 lest, coming suddenly, he find you sleeping. 37 And what I say to you, I say to all: Watch!" (Mark 13:32-37)

Oddly, some interpret verse 32 to mean that they do not need to watch. They foolishly overlook what Jesus said.

Many also misunderstand prophecy.

Yet, in the Continuing Church of God:

> 19 We have also a more sure word of prophecy; whereunto ye do well that ye take heed, as unto a light that shineth in a dark place, until the day dawn, and the day star arise in your hearts: (2 Peter 1:19, KJV)

Prophecy is important.

The Apostle Paul admonished Timothy:

> 2 Preach the word! Be ready in season and out of season. Convince, rebuke, exhort, with all longsuffering and teaching. (2 Timothy 4:2)

Prophecy is a big part of the word of God.

That is a major reason why we write about it in this magazine.

19 PROPHETIC ITEMS to WATCH For in 2019

By Bob Thiel

Jesus said to watch (Mark 13; Luke 21).

There are many events that fall under this category.

Since the sermon I gave in December 2017, titled 18 items to prophetically watch in 2018, world events aligned with all 18 of them. Properly understood biblical prophecies are coming to pass.

So now, let's look at 19 prophetic items to watch for further fulfilment steps in 2019.

1. Scoffers and the Modern Media

The mainstream news media seems to relish promoting then denouncing false prophecies. Many in the alternative media do that as well.

Each year, some make false prophecies related to the Great Tribulation and Jesus' return. Some expect one or both of those events in 2019. Yet, the Great Tribulation will not start then nor will Jesus return in 2019.

Sometimes, false prophecies get significant media attention.

On the other hand, properly understood biblical prophecies, like those in the process of being fulfilled get little media attention--and almost none from 'mainstream' news sources.

Why?

Well, the mainstream media (along with most academics and governmental leaders and internet posters) do not believe the Bible--and even among those who claim to, even less understand and believe biblical prophecies.

The Apostle Peter was inspired to write the following:

> 1 Beloved, I now write to you this second epistle (in both of which I stir up your pure minds by way of reminder), 2 that you may be mindful of the words which were spoken before by the holy prophets, and of the commandment of us, the apostles of the Lord and Savior, 3 knowing this first: that scoffers will come in the last days, walking according to their own lusts, 4 and saying, "Where is the promise of His coming? For since the fathers fell asleep, all things continue as they were from the beginning of creation." 5 For this they willfully forget: that by the word of God the heavens were of old, and the earth standing out of water and in the water, 6 by which the world that then existed perished, being flooded with water. 7 But the heavens and the earth which are now preserved by the same word, are reserved for fire until the day of judgment and perdition of ungodly men.
>
> 8 But, beloved, do not forget this one thing, that with the Lord one day is as a thousand years, and a thousand years as one day. 9 The Lord is not slack concerning His promise, as some count slackness, but is longsuffering toward us, not willing that any should perish but that all should come to repentance. (2 Peter 3:1-9)

It may be of interest to note that part of the mainstream press in the UK covered some of my writings in 2018. They did so with ridicule and failed to mention that what we teach in the Continuing Church of God is coming to pass.

There are many scoffers during these last days.

Many (mainly on the internet) have repeatedly and falsely called me a false prophet and said other bad things about me as well as the Continuing Church of God.

While that turns some away from looking at us, we understand that Jesus said this was to be expected:

> 10 Blessed are those who are persecuted for righteousness' sake, For theirs is the kingdom of heaven. 11 Blessed are you when they revile and persecute you, and say all kinds of evil against you falsely for My sake. 12 Rejoice and be exceedingly glad, for great is your reward in

heaven, for so they persecuted the prophets who were before you (Matthew 5:10-12

We are not to turn away from true understanding of biblical prophecies, but rejoice in going through open doors to proclaim the truth while holding fast to the truth (cf. Revelation 3:7-13).

2. Morality Prophecies Being Fulfilled Daily

Some morality prophecies will be fulfilled daily in 2019, consistent with what the Apostle Paul wrote to the prophetic-evangelist Timothy:

> 1 But know this, that in the last days perilous times will come: 2 For men will be lovers of themselves, lovers of money, boasters, proud, blasphemers, disobedient to parents, unthankful, unholy, 3 unloving, unforgiving, slanderers, without self-control, brutal, despisers of good, 4 traitors, headstrong, haughty, lovers of pleasure rather than lovers of God, 5 having a form of godliness but denying its power. And from such people turn away! 6 For of this sort are those who creep into households and make captives of gullible women loaded down with sins, led away by various lusts, 7 always learning and never able to come to the knowledge of the truth. (2 Timothy 3:1-7)

We see this being fulfilled, not just by terrorists, but by politicians, media experts, academia, and even with scientists.

Like so-called scientists pushing aspects of evolution instead of creation (see also our free booklet, online at www.ccog.org, titled: Is God's Existence Logical?).

Watch for this among leaders and the media, as well as with regular folks.

3. Internet and Other Censorship

More and more governments are putting in procedures and/or laws to restrict what is allowed on the internet. Various forms of media are doing this as well.

Furthermore, then, of course, there is the LBGTQ crowd and those that promote various forms of sexual immorality. The LGBTQ crowd, as well as others who oppose aspects of biblical morality, do not want immoral behaviours labelled as sin.

Since they do not believe what the Bible says about sin, one would think that they would not care that they are considered by Christians as sinful.

Yet, they have been able to silence and/or intimidate many leaders who claim to believe the Bible as well as get laws and court decisions to support them.

Consider also the following:

> 18 For the wrath of God is revealed from heaven against all ungodliness and unrighteousness of men, who suppress the truth in unrighteousness, 19 because what may be known of God is manifest in them, for God has shown it to them. 20 For since the creation of the world His invisible attributes are clearly seen, being understood by the things that are made, even His eternal power and Godhead, so that they are without excuse, 21 because, although they knew God, they did not glorify Him as God, nor were thankful, but became futile in their thoughts, and their foolish hearts were darkened. 22 Professing to be wise, they became fools, 23 and changed the glory of the incorruptible God into an image made like corruptible man — and birds and four-footed animals and creeping things.
>
> 24 Therefore God also gave them up to uncleanness, n the lusts of their hearts, to dishonor their bodies among themselves, 25 who exchanged the truth of God for the lie, and worshiped and served the creature rather than the Creator, who is blessed forever. Amen.
>
> 26 For this reason God gave them up to vile passions. For even their women exchanged the natural use for what is against nature. 27 Likewise also the men, leaving the natural use of the woman, burned in their lust for one another, men with men committing what is shameful, and receiving in themselves the penalty of their error which was due.
>
> 28 And even as they did not like to retain God in their knowledge, God gave them over to a debased mind, to do those things which are not fitting; 29 being filled with all unrighteousness,

> sexual immorality, wickedness, covetousness, maliciousness; full of envy, murder, strife, deceit, evil-mindedness; they are whisperers, 30 backbiters, haters of God, violent, proud, boasters, inventors of evil things, disobedient to parents, 31 undiscerning, untrustworthy, unloving, unforgiving, unmerciful; 32 who, knowing the righteous judgment of God, that those who practice such things are deserving of death, not only do the same but also approve of those who practice them. (Romans 1:18-32)

Notice that the Bible teaches that even approving of forms of sexual immorality is wrong.

The Bible also teaches:

> 11 "Behold, the days are coming," says the Lord God, That I will send a famine on the land, Not a famine of bread, Nor a thirst for water, But of hearing the words of the Lord.
> 12 They shall wander from sea to sea, And from north to east; They shall run to and fro, seeking the word of the Lord, But shall not find it. (Amos 8:11-12)

That does not mean that there will be no Bibles. But the time will come when those promoting various biblical teachings will no longer to be able to have access to the internet, etc. as before. We are seeing more and more of this.

And this especially includes Europe, which has been pressuring social media companies to censor and remove 'offensive' materials.

Watch for moves to restrict rights to object to biblical sins as well as to explain certain biblical prophecies.

4. Weather Sorrows and Troubles

Of course, when thinking about prophecies, most people are concerned about prophecies such as those related to world events, the beginning of sorrows, the four horsemen of the apocalypse, the Great Tribulation, the rise of the Beast/Antichrist/666, Armageddon, etc.

Jesus said:

> 4 And Jesus answered and said to them: "Take heed that no one deceives you. 5 For many will come in My name, saying, 'I am the Christ,' and will deceive many. 6 And you will hear of wars and rumors of wars. See that you are not troubled; for all these things must come to pass, but the end is not yet. 7 For nation will rise against nation, and kingdom against kingdom. And there will be famines, pestilences, and earthquakes in various places. 8 All these are the beginning of sorrows. (Matthew 24:4-8)

> 5 And Jesus, answering them, began to say: "Take heed that no one deceives you. 6 For many will come in My name, saying, 'I am He,' and will deceive many. 7 But when you hear of wars and rumors of wars, do not be troubled; for such things must happen, but the end is not yet. 8 For nation will rise against nation, and kingdom against kingdom. **And there will be earthquakes in various places, and there will be famines and troubles. These are the beginnings of sorrows.** (Mark 13:5-8)

We have seen a lot of 'extreme weather' in various parts of the world in the past few years. Expect more to come:

> 19 Behold, a whirlwind of the Lord has gone forth in fury — A violent whirlwind! It will fall violently on the head of the wicked.
> 20 The anger of the Lord will not turn back Until He has executed and performed the thoughts of His heart. In the latter days you will understand it perfectly. (Jeremiah 23:19-20)

As we get closer to the end, there will be more extreme weather in places.

5. Earthquakes

Jesus taught:

> 7 For nation will rise against nation, and kingdom against kingdom. And there will be famines, pestilences, and earthquakes in various places. (Matthew 24:7).

Expect serious earthquakes in 2019.

Though we will NOT have the earthquake of Revelation 16:18 as that happens during the Day of the Lord, that earthquake will be bigger than what the usual 'experts' have believed was possible. It will change the planet and humble parts of humanity.

But understand, that an earthquake that triggers a massive volcano, such as the USA has in places like Yellowstone and New Zealand has in places like Rotorua, can dramatically change the world. There is also Iceland and the Cascades in the USA.

6. The White Horse of the Apocalypse

The Book of Revelation teaches about riders of four different coloured horses in its sixth chapter.

Notice the following about the first horseman:

> 1 Now I saw when the Lamb opened one of the seals; and I heard one of the four living creatures saying with a voice like thunder, "Come and see." 2 And I looked, and behold, a white horse. He who sat on it had a bow; and a crown was given to him, and he went out conquering and to conquer. (Revelation 6:1-2)

This horseman has to do with spreading false religion. The fact that the horse is white makes the religious message being spread look like it is good.

But the Bible warns about that:

> 12 But what I do, I will also continue to do, that I may cut off the opportunity from those who desire an opportunity to be regarded just as we are in the things of which they boast. 13 For such are false apostles, deceitful workers, transforming themselves into apostles of Christ. 14 And no wonder! For Satan himself transforms himself into an angel of light. 15 Therefore it is no great thing if his ministers also transform themselves into ministers of righteousness, whose end will be according to their works. (2 Corinthians 11:12-15)

Jesus warned about false religion:

> 4 And Jesus answered and said to them: "Take heed that no one deceives you. 5 For many will come in My name, saying, 'I am the Christ,' and will deceive many. (Matthew 24:4-5)

We are seeing the development of an interfaith, ecumenical religion which offers salvation to humanity through a humanistic climate and social agenda.

This is a false gospel. Expect more and more to accept some version of it.

7. Strife and the Red Horse of War

Notice the following:

> 3 When He opened the second seal, I heard the second living creature saying, "Come and see." 4 Another horse, fiery red, went out. And it was granted to the one who sat on it to take peace from the earth, and that people should kill one another; and there was given to him a great sword. (Revelation 6:3-4)

Somewhat paralleling the ride of the second horseman of Revelation 6:3-4, Jesus warned about wars and disturbances:

> 6 And you will hear of wars and rumors of wars. See that you are not troubled; for all these things must come to pass, but the end is not yet. 7 For nation will rise against nation, and kingdom against kingdom. (Matthew 24:6-7a)

"Nation ... against nation" is literally "ethnos ... against ethnos" in the original Greek. Notice how the Orthodox Jewish Bible translates the first half of Matthew 24:7:

> For there will be an intifada of ethnic group against ethnic group,

So, look for ethnic and racial strife in various parts of the world.

We have seen issues with Syria, and more is expected one day (Isaiah 17:1). And let's not overlook Israel and Iran (cf. Isaiah 22:1-14).

8. Trade

Not all warfare is militaristic. There is also economic warfare.

This often involves trade.

The front cover of the January-March 2018 edition of this magazine had the words "Trade War" emblazoned on it.

We saw the start of what many called a trade war in 2018. We also saw the European Union taking on a greater role in setting standards and supporting the role of the World Trade Organization.

Expect more trade issues in 2019.

The Bible shows that Babylonian Europe will dominate trade (cf. Revelation 18:2-3). In 2018, we saw the Europeans making trade-related deals with the Mexicans, Japanese, and Chinese. We also saw them, as well as other nations, upset with the USA and various aspects of its trade and tariff policies.

USA sanctions and tariffs against many nations, including Iran, Russia, and Venezuela, are also driving nations to look to Europe.

Expect to see Europe take more steps to set trading standards with various nations.

9. The Deal of Daniel 9:27

In 2018, we saw the Palestinians state that they could no longer trust the USA to broker a Middle East peace deal.

The Bible teaches that a peace deal will be confirmed for a seven-year period by a European leader who will later rise up and stop animal sacrifices at the midpoint:

> 26 And the people of the prince who is to come Shall destroy the city and the sanctuary. The end of it shall be with a flood, And till the end of the war desolations are determined.
> 27 Then he shall confirm a covenant with many for one week; But in the middle of the week He shall bring an end to sacrifice and offering. And on the wing of abominations shall be one who makes desolate, Even until the consummation, which is determined, Is poured out on the desolate (Daniel 9:26-27).

The 'one week' time element has generally been understood by prophecy watchers to mean a seven year deal (2520 days, based on prophetic 360 day years), that will be broken in the middle of it (after 3 1/2 years). The Hebrew word translated as "week" literally means "sevened" (OT:7620 literal, sevened. Biblesoft's New Exhaustive Strong's Numbers and Concordance with Expanded Greek-Hebrew Dictionary. © 2006).

While Daniel 9:26 calls the leader who confirms the deal a "prince," he is later referred to as the king of the dominating European empire (Daniel 11:40).

One way to show this is a European empire is to realize that it was the people of the Roman Empire of the 1st century that fulfilled the portion of Daniel 9:26 as they destroyed the city (Jerusalem) in 70 A.D.

Jewish sources, while not understanding all of this, also agree that it was Roman forces that destroyed the city and sanctuary as the following demonstrates:

> "The people of the prince will come and destroy the city and the Sanctuary" Daniel 9:26, refers to the Roman legions of Vespasian and Titus, who destroyed Jerusalem. (Daniel 9 – A True Biblical Interpretation. Jews for Judaism. Accessed 07/30/16)

In the 21st century, the European Union includes much of the land and peoples that were part of the ancient Roman Empire. And it is the "prince" coming from that people that verse 27 of Daniel 9 is referring to. Thus, this prophecy tells us that a lower level European leader will somewhat officially start to rise up about 3 ½ years before the great tribulation (and yes, according to Jesus in Matthew 24:9, some "tribulation" does happen prior to the start of the Great Tribulation).

Because of statements and actions by US President Donald Trump, Europeans are even more interested in being part of a Middle East peace deal.

Expect to see, at least some, European efforts along those lines. Especially if we see a major conflict in that region.

Now, once the deal is confirmed for one prophetic week (which could happen sometime AFTER a deal is made) by the "prince," the seven-year countdown for the return of Jesus occurs.

But since the deal is broken in the middle of it, by the King of the North, who was once the "prince" of Daniel 9:26-27, the countdown for the Great Tribulation (Matthew 24:21) will begin.

10. Knowledge Increasing

Notice something from ancient times:

> 6 And the LORD said, "Indeed the people are one and they all have one language, and this is what they begin to do; now nothing that they propose to do will be withheld from them. 7 Come, let Us go down and there confuse their language, that they may not understand one another's speech."
>
> 8 So the LORD scattered them abroad from there over the face of all the earth, and they ceased building the city. 9 Therefore its name is called Babel, because there the Lord confused the language of all the earth; and from there the Lord scattered them abroad over the face of all the earth. (Genesis 11:6-9)

While many languages came out of this, notice another prophecy for the end times:

> 4 "But you, Daniel, shut up the words, and seal the book until the time of the end; many shall run to and fro, and knowledge shall increase." (Daniel 12:4)

We are seeing massive developments in health, robotics, and various sciences.

The arrival and use of automobiles, jet planes, computers, and the internet certainly align with that prophecy.

Computers have also made it easier to communicate, even among people of different languages.

Those who do not accept biblical prophecy seem to consider the knowledge explosion and ability to travel internationally irrelevant.

Yet, those of us who believe it consider this a confirmed prophecy. And this is a prophecy of around 2600 years old!

Expect to see more knowledge developments.

11. Debt

The Bible teaches that the result of debt accumulation will be far worse than even many pessimists believe.

Notice the first part of an end-time prophecy given to the prophet Habakkuk by God over 2600 years ago:

> 2 And the Lord answered me:
> "Write the vision;
> make it plain on tablets,
> so he may run who reads it.
> 3 For still the vision awaits its appointed time;
> it hastens to the end—it will not lie.
> If it seems slow, wait for it;
> it will surely come; it will not delay. (Habakkuk 2:2-3, English Standard Version)

So, this prophecy is so bad that God says people need to take action.

However, many are too puffed up, too arrogant to consider that it will really happen in the 21st century:

> 4 "Behold, his soul is puffed up; it is not upright within him, but the righteous shall live by his faith. 5 "Moreover, wine is a traitor, an arrogant man who is never at rest. His greed is as wide as Sheol; like death he has never enough. He gathers for himself all nations and collects as his own all peoples." (Habakkuk 2:4-5, ESV)

So, a puffed up, arrogant, and greedy people are involved.

This is a people that is heavily indebted:

> 6 Shall not all these take up their taunt against him, with scoffing and riddles for him, and say, "Woe to him who heaps up what is not his own—for how long?—and loads himself with pledges!" (Habakkuk 2:6, ESV)

Treasury bills are a form of pledges that the USA has continued to heap up. The USA is the most indebted nation in the history of humanity and those in it should try to understand this prophecy. Perhaps it should be noted that both the United Kingdom and Canada have very high per capita debt levels.

Notice what will happen:

> 7 Will not your debtors suddenly arise, and those awake who will make you tremble? Then you will be spcil for them. (Habakkuk 2:7, ESV)

When it is time, destruction will be sudden!

Why?

> 8 Because you have plundered many nations,
> all the remnant of the peoples shall plunder you,
> for the blood of man and violence to the earth,
> to cities and all who dwell in them. (Habakkuk 2:8; ESV)

The USA has plundered many nations by borrowing and importing without the intention to truly pay back.

The USA has had violent bloody interventions around the world.

Donald Trump has stated:

I'm the king of debt. I love debt. (Egan M. Donald Trump: 'I'm the king of debt.' CNN, May 7, 2016)

The Bible warns that debt, and having to borrow from foreigners, is a curse that would hit those who received various biblical blessings as they became more disobedient (Deuteronomy 28:15,43-46).

The debt of the USA nearly doubled under the presidency of Barrack Obama and has been increasing under the presidency of Donald Trump.

The economy of the USA has been subsidized by foreign debt for decades now. Without this financing, Americans would think they are poorer than they have been thinking.

The admitted USA national debt is over $21 trillion and expected to exceed $22 trillion this year. And this does not include state or local government debt, corporate debt, or personal debt. The US Congressional Budget Office (CBO) in its 2018 Long-Term Budget Outlook projects even much more debt next decade.

Should interest rates ever rise to historical levels, this will cause massive financial problems for the USA.

When foreigners finally have had enough, it will not end well for the USA.

God told Habakkuk that this should be a very serious matter.

Have you been paying attention to this?

12. US Dollar Dominance will Decrease

Consider the following curse from the Book of Leviticus:

> 19 I will break the pride of your power; (Leviticus 26:19)

While the above undoubtedly has military & economic possibilities, consider that the US dollar is the pride of the USA's power.

It is backed by nothing.

So, it is a prideful thing--plus it does project US power around the world.

Debt, trade, weather, morality, leadership, sanctions, and other issues have given various nations motivations to work to dethrone the US dollar as the world's primary trade and reserve currency.

The economy of the USA has been financed, to a significant degree, by foreigners willing to provide goods to the USA on credit as well as the USA profiting from much of the rest of the world's international trade that is dollar-based.

When the US dollar ceases to be the world's primary reserve currency, there will be massive economic disruption in the USA.

Notice some information about the 'benefits' of being the world's reserve currency:

> Michel Sapin, the French finance minister, called for a "rebalancing" of currencies used in international transactions, implicitly criticizing the status of the U.S. dollar as the principal international reserve currency. Sapin joins a long tradition of French finance ministers criticizing the dollar's privileged status, which goes back to Valery Giscard d'Estaing. In the 1960s, d'Estaing, who served as President of France from 1974 to 1981, said that the United States received an "exorbitant privilege" due to the greenback serving as the basis for much of international financial transactions.
>
> The dollar's global reserve status does confer some real benefits, ...
>
> The purpose of a reserve currency is to help smooth international transactions. Imagine a company that wants to sells goods to a

company in a country with a different currency. When it comes to currency, the companies have two potential problems. First, the exchange rate between the two currencies could shift dramatically and change the price of the good. Secondly, the importing company might use a currency that isn't used much outside of its borders and trading that currency might be difficult. By using a widely circulated currency, such as the U.S. dollar, the two companies eliminate the two risks.

But the two companies whose transactions are smoothed aren't the only ones who benefit. The issuer of the reserve currency, the United States in this case, also benefits. More companies and individuals using the dollar means more transactions denominated in dollars, which provides more liquidity for this currency. Liquidity means that financial assets can be priced more easily and loans are more easily provided. In short, U.S. firms get easier access to capital because of the dollar's reserve status.

These benefits are certainly real and substantial, but there are also costs. ... foreign goods are less expensive to U.S. firms and households, which spurs them to consume cheaper foreign goods and therefore imports increase. (Bunker N. Being the reserve currency has its privileges and costs. July 2014 http://equitablegrowth.org/equitablog/reserve-currency-privileges-costs/ accessed 09/16/17)

Essentially the benefits to the USA have included making money on international trades that the USA otherwise would not be involved in, less inflation, a subsidized economy, lower borrowing cost, a more attractive investment market, and getting many goods from foreign lands at less cost than otherwise.

This status for the USA will not continue.

What happens to the US economy if the Dollar is no longer the reserve currency of the world?

If US T-bills lose their attraction as reserve investments ... it would get harder for the Treasury to sell more of them, requiring higher interest rates to be paid and potentially forcing austerity measures on the US government or triggering classic deficit spending inflation ("printing money" to pay for government, this doesn't happen now because the deficit is financed through sales of those bonds at extremely low interest rates).

If foreign central banks and governments start exchanging their US dollars for some other currency or currencies, then the value of the dollar in international trade drops, it becomes more expensive to buy imported goods in the US and more profitable to sell exported goods from the US. This could have all kinds of political and social effects, especially if the shift was rapid, severe, and unexpected. https://www.quora.com/What-happens-to-the-US-economy-if-the-Dollar-is-no-longer-the-reserve-currency-of-the-world

The above is warning about inflation, higher interest rates, and troubles borrowing. The USA has been essentially on a borrowing binge the last four-five decades and its economy is now dependent upon borrowing.

The time will come when the US dollar is dethroned and this will inflict great pain on the USA. But near the time the US dollar becomes close to worthless, the great tribulation (Matthew 24:21) will come and the USA will then be no more. The Europeans, BRICS's (Brazil, Russia, China, India, South Africa) nations, Iran, Venezuela, Turkey, North Korea, and others want to dethrone the USA dollar.

Dethroning the US dollar will cause massive economic problems for the USA. Much more than almost anyone believes. The standard of living in the USA has been raised/subsidized for years because of the status of the US dollar.

That status is weakening. This will ultimately severely hurt the USA.

13. Cash and 666

Notice the following prophecy:

> 16 He causes all, both small and great, rich and poor, free and slave, to receive a mark on their right hand or on their foreheads, 17 and that no one may buy or sell except one who has the

mark or the name of the beast, or the number of his name.

18 Here is wisdom. Let him who has understanding calculate the number of the beast, for it is the number of a man: His number is 666. (Revelation 13:16-18)

It will be a European power that will fulfill the above prophecy of 666.

It will likely take computers aided with artificial intelligence to aid in the fulfillment of the scriptures in Revelation 13:16-18, as well as cyber-spying/monitoring. I do believe that cyber monitoring will be used by the European Beast, King of the North, 666 power.

We are seeing moves towards digital/electronic money. Knowledge of financial transactions is greatly increasing.

This type of financial surveillance could not have happened during the time of the Apostle John as there was no real way to monitor many financial transactions then. The same was true for all the centuries that followed until the late 20th and now the 21st century. But now not only does the technology exist to monitor most financial transactions, the political will is there as well.

While 2019 will not see a completely cashless world, expect to see more movements towards monitorable payments.

14. Gold

The fall of the US dollar and the trend towards digital money will concern many.

While some economists have called gold a 'relic,' it still has value internationally.

Alex Stanczyk observed:

> Crypto has made its own place in the world by making an amazing leap forward as a medium of exchange, with thus far unrivaled capabilities. But crypto is not gold, and can never be gold. I suggest that BTC and Crypto are better as a medium of exchange, while gold is a better medium for storing value.

This is not because of some dogma I have for the metal. Some will trot out "you are just talking your book" when I mention this.

The simple fact is, out of the near 185,000 tons of estimated above ground gold, someone owns, **all of it**. Every fine gram of gold above ground belongs to someone already, whether that be in the form of bars, coins, jewellery, the thin layer on astronauts helmets that protect them from solar radiation, or the gold plated contacts in the mining rigs used to mine crypto. New gold mined from the ground is usually spoken for before it ever hits a refinery. My job as a physical gold fund manager is not to convince people to buy gold, that job has already been done.

The reason crypto can never replace gold lies in physics: Gold cannot be destroyed

Everything else can. Computers. Exchanges. Mining Pools. Wallets. Powergrids. Internets. Nations. You name it. If you blew up the planet earth, the gold atoms would still be there.

Unlike anything else you can invest or store money in, gold doesn't rely on any external force for this to continue to be true over time. It is sort of like a battery with no expiration date.

Gold exists as atomic number 79 on the periodic table. It is chemically inert and does not interact with oxygen. It is the only element with properties that make it completely immune to the forces of entropy. The only way to destroy it would be to fire it into the sun, or somehow put it in the middle of an equivalent fusion reaction that took the atoms apart at a subatomic level. (Stanczyk A. A Gold Guys View of Crypto, Bitcoin, and Blockchain. Medium.com, December 10, 2017)

Its 'permanence' from a physical perspective is reassuring to many. But the fact it is not a food and provides no calories shows its value has severe limits.

The Bible prophesies that the King of the North will get gold which end time Babylon will also trade with:

37 He shall regard neither the God of his fathers

nor the desire of women, nor regard any god; for he shall exalt himself above them all. 38 But in their place he shall honor a god of fortresses; and a god which his fathers did not know he shall honor with gold and silver, with precious stones and pleasant things. 39 Thus he shall act against the strongest fortresses with a foreign god, which he shall acknowledge, and advance its glory; and he shall cause them to rule over many, and divide the land for gain. 40 "At the time of the end the king of the South shall attack him; and the king of the North shall come against him like a whirlwind, ... 43 He shall have power over the treasures of gold and silver, and over all the precious things of Egypt ... (Daniel 11:37-40,43)

10 ... 'Alas, alas, that great city Babylon, that mighty city! For in one hour your judgment has come.' 11 And the merchants of the earth will weep and mourn over her, for no one buys their merchandise anymore: 12 merchandise of gold and silver, precious stones and pearls, fine linen and purple, silk and scarlet, every kind of citron wood, every kind of object of ivory, every kind of object of most precious wood, bronze, iron, and marble; 13 and cinnamon and incense, fragrant oil and frankincense, wine and oil, fine flour and wheat, cattle and sheep, horses and chariots, and bodies and souls of men. 14 The fruit that your soul longed for has gone from you, and all the things which are rich and splendid have gone from you, and you shall find them no more at all. 15 The merchants of these things, who became rich by her, will stand at a distance for fear of her torment, weeping and wailing, 16 and saying, 'Alas, alas, that great city that was clothed in fine linen, purple, and scarlet, and adorned with gold and precious stones and pearls! (Revelation 18:10-16)

While the Bible is clear that gold will, for a time, not be wanted but tossed (Ezekiel 7:19)—hence it will be worse than useless for a time—it is obvious that into the beginning years of the Great Tribulation (Matthew 24:21-22), which starts in verse 39 of Daniel 11, gold will have value.

Now, understand that Germany has been repatriating gold--and even did so ahead of schedule. Other European nations have repatriated gold as well.

Furthermore, Russia and China have greatly increasing their gold reserves.

Russia, Turkey, and China have been looking to use gold for trade to bypass the USA dollar.

While the price of gold will have ups and downs in 2019, gold will have value after the USA dollar does not.

15. Europe Will Work to Reorganize

The Bible shows that Europe will have problems with truly being united:

41 Whereas you saw the feet and toes, partly of potter's clay and partly of iron, the kingdom shall be divided; yet the strength of the iron shall be in it, just as you saw the iron mixed with ceramic clay. 42 And as the toes of the feet were partly of iron and partly of clay, so the kingdom shall be partly strong and partly fragile. 43 As you saw iron mixed with ceramic clay, they will mingle with the seed of men; but they will not adhere to one another, just as iron does not mix with clay. (Daniel 2:41-43)

Expect to see problems, as well as opportunities, with European unity in 2019.

Despite problems, the Bible also shows that Europe will reorganize:

12 The ten horns which you saw are ten kings who have received no kingdom as yet, but they receive authority for one hour as kings with the beast. 13 These are of one mind, and they will give their power and authority to the beast. (Revelation 17:12-13).

Various ones are calling for a version of that in Europe. Even Pope Francis has called for Europe to be creative and think beyond national boundaries. Some have specifically called for a "United States of Europe."

The idea of a United States of Europe has been something that Church of God leaders have written about for decades.

The prophesied reorganizations in Revelation 17:12-13

will not happen in 2019, but expect calls to reorganize Europe and improve European unity.

16. Europe Will Develop its Military

The Bible shows that Europe will become a major military power:

> 24 He shall enter peaceably, even into the richest places of the province; and he shall do what his fathers have not done, nor his forefathers: he shall disperse among them the plunder, spoil, and riches; and he shall devise his plans against the strongholds, but only for a time. 25 He shall stir up his power and his courage against the king of the South with a great army. (Daniel 11:24-25)

Notice that the 'he,' which is a European power, will first seem peaceful, but will end up having a great army!

Europe is working on developing its own army. It even has an umbrella structure called PESCO (PErmanent STructured COoperation). Nearly all the EU nations are officially part of PESCO. The plan is to develop military technology and a unified European military.

One that is independent of the USA.

Furthermore, Europe has been working on technology, like the Large Hadron Collider and its Galileo satellite system, in order to give it capabilities independent of the USA.

Europe has been getting it Galileo satellites launched and expects to be fully operational in 2020.

This is a trend to watch. Germany will take steps to promote a stronger military.

While most do not believe that Europe can or ever will destroy the USA, consider the following prophecies:

> 5 "Woe to Assyria, the rod of My anger And the staff in whose hand is My indignation. 6 I will send him against an ungodly nation, And against the people of My wrath I will give him charge, To seize the spoil, to take the prey, And to tread them down like the mire of the streets. 7 Yet he does not mean so, Nor does his heart think so; But it is in his heart to destroy, And cut off not a few nations. ... 11 As I have done to Samaria and her idols, Shall I not do also to Jerusalem and her idols?' 12 Therefore it shall come to pass, when the Lord has performed all His work on Mount Zion and on Jerusalem, that He will say, "I will punish the fruit of the arrogant heart of the king of Assyria, and the glory of his haughty looks."(Isaiah 10:5-7,11-12).

> 39 Thus he shall act against the strongest fortresses with a foreign god, which he shall acknowledge, and advance its glory; and he shall cause them to rule over many, and divide the land for gain. (Daniel 11:39)

In Isaiah 10, the reference to "Assyria" is pointing to a German-dominated European power in the 21st century. The reference to "Samaria" is pointing to the USA in the 21st century.

Related to Daniel 11:39, consider that in the 21st century, it is the USA with the strongest fortresses. The power with the strongest fortresses will be taken over by the European Beast power. Technology, as well as deception, will be factors in the military takeover of the USA.

This will cause the world to marvel:

> 3 And I saw one of his heads as if it had been mortally wounded, and his deadly wound was healed. And all the world marveled and followed the beast. 4 So they worshiped the dragon who gave authority to the beast; and they worshiped the beast, saying, "Who is like the beast? Who is able to make war with him?" (Revelation 13:3-4)

People will be shocked when Europe shows it is a militarily successful power. It is now taking steps that will lead to the fulfillment of various warring prophecies.

But it is too soon for the USA to be taken over in 2019. There are still other events (like the confirmation of the deal of Daniel 9:27) that still must take place first (cf. Matthew 24:4-16).

With Europeans concerned about the USA and NATO, expect more steps by the EU to develop a powerful military.

17. Steps Towards the Formation of the King of the South Will Occur

The formation of the King of the South is something to look out for.

Psalm 83 prophesies a confederacy:

> 3 They have taken crafty counsel against Your people, And consulted together against Your sheltered ones. 4 They have said, "Come, and let us cut them off from being a nation, That the name of Israel may be remembered no more." 5 For they have consulted together with one consent; They form a confederacy against You: 6 The tents of Edom and the Ishmaelites; Moab and the Hagrites; 7 Gebal, Ammon, and Amalek;Philistia with the inhabitants of Tyre; 8 Assyria also has joined with them; They have helped the children of Lot. (Psalm 83:3-8)

Most of the peoples listed above are currently in the Middle East and North Africa, with the exception of Assyria--which is mainly in Europe.

Notice that a deal is alluded to in Daniel 11 and will be broken:

> 15 ... the king of the North ... 25 ... the king of the South ... 27 Both these kings' hearts shall be bent on evil, and they shall speak lies at the same table; but it shall not prosper, for the end will still be at the appointed time. (Daniel 11:15,25,27)

So, these powers will have made lying deals.

After the USA is taken over (Daniel 11:39), they will then turn on each other:

> 40 "At the time of the end the king of the South shall attack him; and the king of the North shall come against him like a whirlwind, with chariots, horsemen, and with many ships; and he shall enter the countries, overwhelm them, and pass through. 41 He shall also enter the Glorious Land, and many countries shall be overthrown; but these shall escape from his hand: Edom, Moab, and the prominent people of Ammon. 42 He shall stretch out his hand against the countries, and the land of Egypt shall not escape. 43 He shall have power over the treasures of gold and silver, and over all the precious things of Egypt; also the Libyans and Ethiopians shall follow at his heels. (Daniel 11:40-43)

US and European politicians have called for a confederation or coalition of nations in the Middle East and North Africa to suppress terrorism as well as deal with migrant issues.

Saudi Arabia, Egypt, and others have taken steps that will help the ultimate formation of the King of the South.

There now is a military alliance among most Muslim nations in the Middle East and North Africa. There has even been a call from the USA for a Middle East-North Africa "Arab NATO." The Bible tells of a coming confederacy coming to those lands.

While the confederacy is not expected be fully formed in 2019, watch for events that will point in its direction. A King of the South will arise, be involved in some deals, later do damage, and later be destroyed (see also Ezekiel 30:1-8).

18. The Time of the Gentiles will Lead to Armageddon

The New Testament teaches:

> 24 ... Jerusalem will be trampled by Gentiles until the times of the Gentiles are fulfilled. (Luke 21:24)

> 2 But leave out the court which is outside the temple, and do not measure it, for it has been given to the Gentiles. And they will tread the holy city underfoot for forty-two months. (Revelation 11:2)

More Gentile-dominated groups and projects are appearing to get the world to move away from an Anglo-American dominated world order. Basically, part of the objective of the BRICS, EAEU (Eurasian Economic Union), Shanghai Cooperation Organization, and even the European Union is to establish a new world order—one no longer dominated by the USA and its Anglo-Saxon allies, like the UK.

Some few years after that new order is in place in

Europe, Eurasian powers will take military steps against it:

> 16 Now the number of the army of the horsemen was two hundred million; I heard the number of them. 17 And thus I saw the horses in the vision: those who sat on them had breastplates of fiery red, hyacinth blue, and sulfur yellow; and the heads of the horses were like the heads of lions; and out of their mouths came fire, smoke, and brimstone. (Revelation 9:16-17)

> 13 And I saw three unclean spirits like frogs coming out of the mouth of the dragon, out of the mouth of the beast, and out of the mouth of the false prophet. 14 For they are spirits of demons, performing signs, which go out to the kings of the earth and of the whole world, to gather them to the battle of that great day of God Almighty. 15 "Behold, I am coming as a thief. Blessed is he who watches, and keeps his garments, lest he walk naked and they see his shame." 16 And they gathered them together to the place called in Hebrew, Armageddon. (Revelation 16:13-16).

It is only a force which includes significant involvement with Asia that could put together an army so massive in the 21st century. Actually, when the above was written in the 1st century, there were not even believed to be that many males on planet Earth. But there are clearly enough now.

Consider, further, that with its One Belt, One Road (AKA Silk Road) project, China is working on making roads that will transport troops to Armageddon. China has over 60 nations involved and, on an inflation-adjusted basis, is expected to pour ten times the amount of money into this than the USA did for its Marshall Plan, which mainly helped 6 European nations.

The gathering of Armageddon will not happen in 2019, but some events to make that gathering happen will.

19. Jews Ready to Sacrifice

The Bible teaches the following:

> 27 Then he shall confirm a covenant with many for one week; But in the middle of the week He shall bring an end to sacrifice and offering. And on the wing of abominations shall be one who makes desolate, Even until the consummation, which is determined, Is poured out on the desolate (Daniel 9:27).

> 31 And forces shall be mustered by him, and they shall defile the sanctuary fortress; then they shall take away the daily sacrifices, and place there the abomination of desolation. (Daniel 11:31)

Now, in order for the sacrifices to stop, they must start.

Essentially, since the destruction of Jerusalem and what is called the Second Temple in A.D. 70, the Jews stopped sacrificing animals.

Some claim that this will require what is called a Third Temple in Jerusalem.

Because of Donald Trump's decision on December 6, 2017 related to recognizing Jerusalem as Israel's capital and the move of the US Embassy to Jerusalem in 2018, some think this will make it easier for a 'Third Temple' to be built there.

Some have claimed that Donald Trump is a new Cyrus.

But unlike Cyrus (Isaiah 44:24-28, 45:1-4), Donald Trump was not prophesied by name to get a Jewish temple rebuilt.

Nor is a Third Temple in Jerusalem needed for animal sacrifices to resume.

Right now, all the Jews are waiting on is for official government permission.

Biblically, they do NOT need a rebuilt Temple to sacrifice. They only need an altar, a qualified priest, and implements.

Groups like the Temple Institute and Reconstituted Sanhedrin claim to have all of that.

Notice that the Bible recorded the following:

> 6 From the first day of the seventh month began they to offer burnt offerings unto the LORD. But the foundation of the temple of the LORD was

not yet laid. (Ezra 3:6)

One may argue that since it takes the participation of Jewish religious leaders in order for Jewish animal sacrifices to be resumed, that the above scripture is a moot point.

As it turns out, representatives of both the Sanhedrin and the Temple Institute have told me that they only need government permission to sacrifice, as they are basically otherwise prepared.

So, despite what may happen in Jerusalem with the area called the Temple Mount, the Jews will one day reinstitute animal sacrifices and they do not need a Third Temple to do that.

The Fulfillment of Matthew 28:19-20 and Matthew 24:14

An item that the CCOG will be working on will be Matthew 28:19-20 and Matthew 24:14.

Jesus taught:

> 19 Go therefore and make disciples of all the nations, baptizing them in the name of the Father and of the Son and of the Holy Spirit, 20 teaching them to observe all things that I have commanded you; and lo, I am with you always, even to the end of the age. (Matthew 28:19-20)

In the Continuing Church of God sermons, I have gone over everything that the Bible records that Jesus spoke in the New Testament.

Additionally, this is something I instructed our ministers in Africa and Europe to do while visiting them in Nairobi, Kenya in February 2017.

We also have made literature available, not only on the internet, but in printed form and in multiple languages.

Jesus also taught:

> **14 And this gospel of the kingdom will be preached in all the world as a witness to all the nations, and then the end will come.** 15 "Therefore when you see the 'abomination of desolation,' spoken of by Daniel the prophet, standing in the holy place" (whoever reads, let him understand), 16 then let those who are in Judea flee to the mountains. 17 Let him who is on the housetop not go down to take anything out of his house. 18 And let him who is in the field not go back to get his clothes. 19 But woe to those who are pregnant and to those who are nursing babies in those days! 20 And pray that your flight may not be in winter or on the Sabbath. 21 For then there will be great tribulation, such as has not been since the beginning of the world until this time, no, nor ever shall be. 22 And unless those days were shortened, no flesh would be saved; but for the elect's sake those days will be shortened. (Matthew 24 14-22)

Notice that the Great Tribulation happens after Matthew 24:14 has been fulfilled to God's satisfaction.

In the Continuing Church of God, we have a booklet, The Gospel of the Kingdom of God, available in close to 100 languages. They can be found at www.ccog.org

According to AWStats, our websites have been visited by people from at least 220 nations/territories. According to YouTube our online videos have been viewed by people from at least 220 nations/territories.

More will be done.

The late artist Andy Warhol was known for getting the idea out that people are entitled to their "fifteen minutes of fame."

The Apostle Paul wrote that God would have a short work:

> 28 For He will finish the work and cut it short in righteousness, Because the Lord will make a short work upon the earth. (Romans 9:28)

In the Continuing Church of God, we are preparing for this through the development of articles and booklets, and in numerous languages.

We believe that when we publicly identify the coming King of the North and explain that he is pushing a false peace and false gospel, and that he will destroy the USA and its Anglo-Saxon dominated allies, as well as an Islamic power, that media attention will be focused on us and what we teach.

This will be the short work, and will lead to the fulfillment of Matthew 24:14.

Are you going to watch or support the work?

Jesus praised the Philadelphians for their work (Revelation 3:7-13), while condemning the Laodicean Christians for being lukewarm about the work (Revelation 3:14-22).

But when will the end come?

When God determines that Matthew 24:14 has been fulfilled, and we of the Continuing Church of God continue to diligently work on this.

Summary

Many events we have seen in the 21st century align with a proper understanding of Bible prophecy.

Notice what Jesus said:

> 33 Take heed, watch and pray; for you do not know when the time is. 34 It is like a man going to a far country, who left his house and gave authority to his servants, and to each his work, and commanded the doorkeeper to watch. 35 Watch therefore, for you do not know when the master of the house is coming — in the evening, at midnight, at the crowing of the rooster, or in the morning — 36 lest, coming suddenly, he find you sleeping. 37 And what I say to you, I say to all: Watch! (Mark 13:33-37)

This article has given you at least 19 things to watch for in 2019, while we work on Matthew 24:14 and 28:19-20.

FREE *Continuing Church of God* Books and Booklets
at www.ccog.org/books

Christians: AMBASSADORS

Continuing History of the Church of God

Dating: A Key to Success in Marriage

Faith for Those God has Called and Chosen

The Gospel of the Kingdom of God

Is God Calling You?

Is God's Existence Logical?

Prayer: What Does the Bible Teach?

The SECOND Commandment

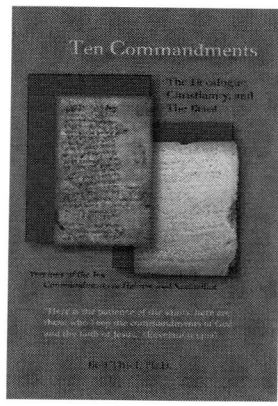

By Bob Thiel

Should you pay attention to the second commandment?

While you may think that you would not be guilty of violating the second commandment, it is commonly violated.

Part of the reason why is because humans, apart from God, are truly carnally minded:

> 5 For those who live according to the flesh set their minds on the things of the flesh, but those who live according to the Spirit, the things of the Spirit. 6 For to be carnally minded is death, but to be spiritually minded is life and peace. 7 Because the carnal mind is enmity against God; for it is not subject to the law of God, nor indeed can be. 8 So then, those who are in the flesh cannot please God. (Romans 8:5-8)

Yet, the carnally-minded think that they can please God through the veneration of idols and icons.

The carnal mind wants something to help worship God, like something physical to remind him of the invisible God. This type of item is forbidden in the second commandment.

The second commandment from the Book of Exodus states:

> 4 "You shall not make for yourself a carved image — any likeness of anything that is in heaven above, or that is in the earth beneath, or that is in the water under the earth; 5 you shall not bow down to them nor serve them. For I, the Lord your God, am a jealous God, visiting the iniquity of the fathers upon the children to the third and fourth generations of those who hate Me, 6 but showing mercy to thousands, to those who love Me and keep My commandments. (Exodus 20:4-6)

Jesus warned:

> 22 You worship what you do not know; we know what we worship, for salvation is of the Jews. 23 But the hour is coming, and now is, when the true worshipers will worship the Father in spirit and truth; for the Father is seeking such to worship Him. 24 God is Spirit, and those who worship Him must worship in spirit and truth. (John 4:22-24)

People accept idols, icons, and traditions as superior to the word of God and then do not worship God in truth. God only wants people to worship Him in spirit and in truth!

Those who really know the true Creator God as their Father do not need a picture or icon to assist with prayer. One who believes otherwise has not come to know God — and is not filled with and led by the Spirit of God. In order to worship God in spirit, you must have His Holy Spirit. "Now if anyone does not have the Spirit of Christ, he is not His" (Romans 8:9).

God gives His Holy Spirit after repentance, baptism, and laying on of hands (Acts 2:38; 8:16-17) — and only to those who OBEY Him (Acts 5:32).

Consider the following from the New Jerusalem Bible (a Catholic translation):

> 4 Draw me out of the net they have spread for me, for you are my refuge; 5 to your hands I commit my spirit, by you have I been redeemed. God of truth, 6 you hate those who serve useless idols; but my trust is in Yahweh: (Psalm 31:4-6. NJB)

The God of truth hates worship with idols.
Now, you may tell yourself that your veneration of the cross, saints, etc. is the religion of your ancestors

and hence is acceptable. But that is wrong.

Melito of Sardis ran into similar arguments in the second century:

> How can the unseen God be sculptured? Nay, it is the likeness of thyself that thou makest and worshippest. Because the wood has been sculptured, hast thou not the insight to perceive that it is still wood, or that the stone is still stone? The gold also the workman: taketh according to its weight in the balance. And when thou hast had it made into an image, why dose thou weigh it? Therefore thou art a lover of gold, and not a lover of God...
>
> Again, there are persons who say: Whatsoever our fathers have bequeathed to us, that we reverence. Therefore, of course, it is, that those whose fathers have bequeathed them poverty strive to become rich! and those whose fathers did not instruct them, desire to be instructed, and to learn that which their fathers knew not! And why, forsooth, do the children of the blind see, and the children of the lame walk? Nay, it is not well for a man to follow his predecessors, if they be those whose course was evil; but rather that we should turn from that path of theirs, lest that which befell our predecessors should bring disaster upon us also...
>
> And then shall those who have not known God, and those who have made them idols, bemoan themselves, when they shall see those idols of theirs being burnt up, together with themselves, and nothing shall be found to help them. (Melito. A Discourse Which Was in the Presence of Antoninus Caesar)

While many people consider Melito to be a saint, many ignore his warning against idols and tradition. Jesus warned against putting traditions above God's commandments (Matthew 15:3-9) and putting family considerations above following Him (Matthew 10:37).

Many supposedly 'Christian' symbols are from idolatrous paganism. Many people combine pagan worship practices, which the Apostle Paul warns about as follows:

> 19 What am I saying then? That an idol is anything, or what is offered to idols is anything? 20 Rather, that the things which the Gentiles sacrifice they sacrifice to demons and not to God, and I do not want you to have fellowship with demons. 21 You cannot drink the cup of the Lord and the cup of demons; you cannot partake of the Lord's table and of the table of demons. (1 Corinthians 10:19-21)

Christians should keep God's Holy Days and not observe compromised pagan substitutes (for more information on this, please check out our booklet Should You Observe God's Holy Days or Demonic Holidays?).

The Bible teaches that God made humankind in His image (Genesis 1:27). Yet, it also teaches against humans making figures of God according to their image or imagination or seeing physical objects (Deuteronomy 4:15-19).

It may be of interest to note that many of the most commonly used pictures of Jesus are actually believed to have originally been an attempt to make Jesus look like a younger version of Zeus (Taylor J. What did Jesus really look like? BBC, December 24, 2015).

Christians are to "walk by faith, not by sight" (2 Corinthians 5:7), yet like the pagans of old, many are excessively awed by colorful images (Ezekiel 23:14-16; 1 Kings 12:28-31) and stubbornly cling to various forms of idolatry (cf. 1 Samuel 15:23).

Modern Idols?

Now, you may not bow down before crosses, deities, or saints. But could you be making your job, social status, money, appetite, or possessions your idol?

Many people do.

People will worship modern idols by covetously seeking possessions, status, money, or many such things.

Notice that this truly is a form of idolatry:
> 5 Therefore put to death your members which are on the earth: fornication, uncleanness, passion, evil desire, and covetousness, which is

idolatry. (Colossians 3:5, NKJV)

5 So put to death the sinful, earthly things lurking within you. Have nothing to do with sexual immorality, impurity, lust, and evil desires. Don't be greedy, for a greedy person is an idolater, worshiping the things of this world. (Colossians 3:5. NLT)

There is a reason that the Bible warns:

10 For the love of money is a root of all kinds of evil, for which some have strayed from the faith in their greediness, and pierced themselves through with many sorrows. (1 Timothy 6:10)

Money, of itself, is not evil—but breaking the commandments is.

Loving the physical above God is a modern type of idolatry.

Consider also the following:

16 Now behold, one came and said to Him, "Good Teacher, what good thing shall I do that I may have eternal life?"

17 So He said to him, "Why do you call Me good? No one is good but One, that is, God. But if you want to enter into life, keep the commandments."

18 He said to Him, "Which ones?"

Jesus said, "'You shall not murder,' 'You shall not commit adultery,' 'You shall not steal,' 'You shall not bear false witness,' 19 'Honor your father and your mother,' and, 'You shall love your neighbor as yourself.'"

20 The young man said to Him, "All these things I have kept from my youth. What do I still lack?"

21 Jesus said to him, "If you want to be perfect, go, sell what you have and give to the poor, and you will have treasure in heaven; and come, follow Me."

22 But when the young man heard that saying, he went away sorrowful, for he had great possessions. (Matthew 19:16-22)

The young man thought he kept the Ten Commandments, but his attachment to the physical showed he did not "seek first the kingdom of God" (Matthew 6:33) and was guilty of covetous idolatry.

It is not that holding possessions has to be a problem (Abraham, Isaac, Jacob, and King David were all wealthy), but this man may have had an opportunity to be an apostle or hold some other leadership role. Yet, let his possessions get in his way.

Do your possessions get in the way?

While you may not think you are as important as a king or ancient patriarch, "it is better to be a doorkeeper in the house of My God" (Psalm 84:10) than to make an idol of your possessions (cf. Luke 12:15).

Some will work on the Sabbath and/or Holy Days because they idolize their job or paycheck.

Some will not give tithes and/or sufficient offerings because of their attachment to them and their lack of faith in the true God.

Consider that Jesus said:

20 Fool! 21 ... is he who lays up treasure for himself, and is not rich toward God." (Luke 12:20-21)

Although God's plan does include repentant idolaters (cf. Isaiah 42:16-18) venerating statues/icons or coveting possessions is idolatry and is not being rich towards God.

As cited earlier, 1 Samuel 15:22-23 teaches that stubbornness is as idolatry. In Deuteronomy 21:20, the Bible ties gluttony and being a drunkard in with stubbornness. Be careful that your eating and drinking practices are not a form of idolatry.

Second Commandment Before Sinai, from Jesus, and After Jesus' Death

The Bible shows the second commandment was in

place before Mt. Sinai:

"'Put away the foreign gods that are among you, purify yourselves'...So they gave Jacob all the foreign gods which were in their hands, and the earrings which were in their ears and Jacob hid them" (Genesis 35:2,4). "And you shall not let any of your descendants pass through the fire of Molech ... for all these abominations the men of the land have done, who were before you, and thus the land is defiled" (Leviticus 18:21,27). "If I have observed the sun when it shines, or the moon moving in its brightness, so that my heart has been secretly enticed, and my mouth has kissed my hand; This also would be an iniquity deserving of judgement, For I would have denied God who is above" (Job 31:26-28) (note this is believed to be part of idol worship).

Jesus taught and expanded the second commandment:

"You shall worship the LORD your God, and Him only you shall serve" (Matthew 4:10). "You shall worship the LORD your God, and Him only you shall serve" (Luke 4:8). "God is spirit, and those who worship Him must worship in spirit and truth" (John 4:24). "But I have a few things against you, because you have there those who hold the doctrine of Balaam...to eat things sacrificed to idols" (Revelation 2:14). "Nevertheless, I have a few things against you, because you allow...My servants to...eat things sacrificed to idols" (Revelation 2:20).

After Jesus was resurrected, the New Testament taught the second commandment:

"we write to them to abstain from things polluted by idols" (Acts 15:20). "Now while Paul waited for them in Athens, his spirit was provoked within him when he saw that the city was given over to idols...Then Paul stood in the midst of the Areopagus and said...'God, who made the world and everything in it, since He is Lord of heaven and earth, does not dwell in temples made with hands. Nor is He worshipped with men's hands, as though He needed anything'" (Acts 17:16,22,24-25). "Professing to be wise, they became fools, and changed the glory of the incorruptible God into an image made like corruptible man--and birds and four footed animals and creeping things" (Romans 1:22-23). "But now I have written to you not to keep company with anyone named a brother, who is...an idolater" (1 Corinthians 5:11). "Neither... idolators...will inherit the kingdom of God" (1 Corinthians 6:9-10). "And do not become idolaters as were some of them... Therefore, my beloved, flee from idolatry" (1 Corinthians 10:7,14). "And what agreement has the temple of God with idols?" (2 Corinthians 6:16). "Now the works of the flesh are evident... idolatry" (Galatians 5:19,20). "For this you know that no ... idolater, has any inheritance in the kingdom of Christ and God" (Ephesians 5:5). "Therefore put to death...covetousness, which is idolatry" (Colossians 3:5). "you turned to God from idols" (1 Thessalonians 1:9). "abominable idolatries" (1 Peter 4:3). "Little children, keep yourselves from idols" (1 John 5:21). "But I have a few things against you, because you have there those who hold the doctrine of Balaam... to eat things sacrificed to idols" (Revelation 2:14). "Nevertheless, I have a few things against you, because you allow...My servants to...eat things sacrificed to idols" (Revelation 2:20). "But the rest of mankind, who were not killed by these plagues, did not repent of the works of their hands, that they should not worship demons, and idols of gold, silver, brass, stone, and wood, which can neither see nor hear nor walk" (Revelation 9:20). "But ...idolaters...shall have their part in the lake which burns with fire and brimstone, which is the second death" (Revelation 21:8). "But outside are...idolaters" (Revelation 22:15).

While the New Testament does not explicitly state not to bow down to graven images, it does teach that idolatry is wrong and that covetousness is a form of idolatry.

Furthermore, the New Testament expands on the second commandment by explaining that it also includes covetousness and that God only wants to be worshiped in truth. No idol or icon is true to God nor should be bowed before.

STUDY THE BIBLE COURSE

Lesson 14c: What is Man?

Bob Thiel, Editor-in-Chief
Published 2019 by the Continuing Church of God

> Preface: This course is highly based upon the personal correspondence course developed in 1954 that began under the direction of the late C. Paul Meredith in the old Radio Church of God. Various portions have been updated for the 21st century (though much of the original writing has been retained). It also has more scriptural references, as well as information and questions not in the original course. Unless otherwise noted, scriptural references are to the NKJV, copyright Thomas Nelson Publishing, used by permission. The KJV, sometimes referred to as the Authorized Version is also often used. Additionally, Catholic-approved translations such as the New Jerusalem Bible (NJB) are sometimes used as are other translations.

This is the third part of this lesson. The previous parts were in earlier editions of this magazine.

The Spirit in Man

1. Since no person has an immortal soul which lives on apart from the body after death — a person basically IS a soul. But does the Bible speak elsewhere of A SPIRIT IN MAN? 1 Corinthians 2:9-14. Notice especially verse 11.

2. Is this spirit the person — or is it something that is in the person? Verse 11.

3. Does God form this spirit WITHIN each human being? Zechariah 12:1.

COMMENT: This spirit is NOT THE PERSON — it is something that is IN a person. Connected with the physical brain (matter) of the person, it forms human MIND. It merely imparts humanity's unique power of intellect and personality.

Satan does not represent this spirit as merely something that is IN the person. Long ago, Satan palmed it off as an immortal soul. Satan led people to believe this spirit IS the person, not something IN the person. Satan then led humans to believe the BODY is merely the HOUSE in which the HUMAN (falsely represented as an immortal soul) dwells.

The spirit that is IN a human has no consciousness OF ITSELF. It cannot KNOW, apart from the physical brain. It cannot SEE, of itself. Coupled with the brain, it can see only through the physical eye. It cannot hear without the human ear.

PROOF: A blind man has this human spirit IN him — but it sees NOTHING. This spirit is IN a deaf woman. But she cannot hear, though she has full powers of MIND otherwise.

Since this spirit cannot see without a functioning physical eye, nor hear without a properly functioning physical ear, in a LIVING human, it most certainly cannot see or hear apart from a DEAD human.

Neither can it KNOW or THINK apart from the physical brain. By a physical drug the physical brain may be rendered unconscious. This drug cannot affect the spirit in the person — yet the person KNOWS NOTHING while the brain is rendered unconscious, even though the spirit is still in the person.

Thus, as the Bible plainly says, dead men "know nothing" (Ecclesiastes 9:5). This spirit is not the person. It is merely something IN the person which imparts intellect or MIND power to the brain. It is NOT a ghost. It is spirit ESSENCE. It is merely an ingredient added to the brain which produces human MIND. It is a HUMAN spirit. The person with this spirit can know only PHYSICAL things. It requires the addition of ANOTHER Spirit – God's HOLY Spirit – to open the human mind to comprehension of spiritual things (1 Corinthians 2:9-10).

GOD says that what came from the dust was the human. Satan deceives people into believing that what came from the ground was NOT the HUMAN, but the HOUSE in which the human dwells – the GARMENT the person wears – the PRISON which holds the "immortal soul" captive!

Jesus Christ said, "That which is born of the flesh [matter from the ground] IS FLESH [matter from dust]" (John 3:6). Nowhere does the Bible say man IS a spirit. It says man is mortal. It says the soul that sins shall DIE (Ezekiel 18:20).

Jesus Christ said a person may be BORN AGAIN – next time, born of GOD, who is a SPIRIT (John 3:3-7). THEN, He said, we shall BE SPIRIT. But now we are FLESH! Christ came to reveal the HOPE of humanity – to be BORN of GOD, by a resurrection from the dead. Born into the very GOD FAMILY. That is what salvation is! Satan has blinded a deceived world from this GREAT HOPE! He seeks to destroy all this, deceiving men into believing man is already immortal – an "immortal soul" that can't die – could not be resurrected from the DEAD!

Thus Satan seeks to destroy the Gospel! Satan represents the "spirit in man" as being, itself, the conscious MAN. The true FACT is, the "spirit IN man" merely imparts certain characteristics to the physical BRAIN.

4. What does the spirit in man add to man's brain? 1 Corinthians 2:11.

COMMENT: It is this spirit that is IN man, which, added to material BRAIN, gives this human brain the functions of MIND. But this Scripture PLAINLY says that this spirit is merely something that is IN the MAN. It is NOT the MAN!

This spirit IN man cannot, of itself, see anything. The human BRAIN SEES through the human physical EYE. It hears through the physical ear. The spirit in man cannot know, or think, or remember, OF ITSELF. Of itself, it has no consciousness. It merely IMPARTS human mind-powers and personality to the human brain.

A man dies, and in that very day his thinking stops, his thoughts cease (Psalm 146:4). Dead people are totally unconscious – they know nothing (Ecclesiastes 9:5). At death, this spirit has no consciousness – it SLEEPS (1 Corinthians 11:30; 15:51; 1 Thessalonians 4:14).

But this spirit is NOT the "soul." That which God formed out of material dust became the soul! THE SOUL IS MATERIAL – NOT SPIRITUAL.

This HUMAN spirit imparts to the human brain the power of MIND. Without it, no man could comprehend HUMAN knowledge WHICH IS WHOLLY PHYSICAL AND MATERIAL KNOWLEDGE. This knowledge is confined to that which enters the mind through the five sensory channels. But such a mind STILL cannot comprehend spiritual knowledge.

5. How, then, can man know and understand SPIRITUAL things? 1 Corinthians 2:11. Be sure to read this verse in its context.

COMMENT: Spiritual things cannot be seen with the eye, heard with the ear, felt with the hands. The greatest minds – scientific, philosophical minds – cannot really come to know and understand SPIRITUAL truths.

Just as no animal BRAIN, without this human SPIRIT that is IN the person, can have MIND and comprehension of PHYSICAL knowledge on the HUMAN plane; even so, no HUMAN MIND can have true comprehension of spiritual things on the DIVINE plane, unless or until the HOLY SPIRIT of GOD has been imparted to this human mind.

Satan has deceived the whole world into counterfeiting this human spirit, and representing it as an immortal soul. THAT IS SATAN'S LIE!

How to Receive Eternal Life

Human are physical beings, POSSESSING ONLY PHYSICAL LIFE. If someone is to live forever and CAN CLAIM THE PROMISES MADE TO ABRAHAM, that person must acquire ETERNAL life. But how?

1. Is eternal life a GIFT that God must bestow upon humans? Romans 6:23.

2. What did Jesus answer the young man who asked how to obtain this gift of eternal life? Matthew 19:17. Is keeping God's commandments a requirement?

3. Is obedience to God necessary in order to receive the Holy Spirit – the POWER which imparts to us the gift of eternal life? Compare Acts 5:32 with Acts 2:38. Notice also Romans 8:11.

COMMENT: Even though we obey God while composed of earthly flesh, that obedience does not earn or impart eternal life. Obedience is a CONDITION to continued receipt of the Holy Spirit (incorrectly translated as "Holy Ghost" in the KJV) – the POWER by which we are raised from the dead to eternal life – to immortality! (1 Corinthians 15:44, 50-54.)

We must be raised from the dead. We must be born again – born of God who is Spirit (John 4:24) in order to gain immortality.

4. When we are raised from the dead and born – born again from above – of what are we to be composed – of spirit? John 3:6. How does this compare with 1 Corinthians 15:44-46?

COMMENT: BEING BORN OF THE SPIRIT IS NOT A REFORMING OF AN IMMORTAL SOUL we are now supposed to possess – but a NEW BIRTH. That is the reason Jesus said, "You must be born again" (John 3:7). You must be raised from the dead. Through a resurrection, and simultaneously BEING BORN OF THE SPIRIT, YOU WILL then HAVE a body of spirit – ETERNALLY LIVING Spirit – and NOT one of fleshly protoplasm subject to death! You will be born as an immortal spirit into THE VERY FAMILY OF GOD (Ephesians 3:15 and Hebrews 12:9).

Only God Is Immortal!

Many still twist all of these Bible passages about death and apply them to the body, clinging to the pagan idea that they now possess an immortal soul. Let us notice how the Bible uses the words "immortal" and "immortality."

1. Where is the only place in the (NKJV/DRB) Bible that the word "immortal" appears? 1 Timothy 1:17.

COMMENT: This verse refers to Jesus Christ, the world's coming King, who was made immortal and very God through a resurrection to eternal life.

2. According to 1 Timothy 6:16, who is the only one born of woman that has immortality?

3. Who brought to MANKIND the knowledge of how to achieve eternal life and immortality? 2 Timothy 1:10. Does this verse indicate that immortality is something someone already has? Through what was immortality brought to light? Same verse. Isn't part of the Gospel, then, the good news about how to gain immortality?

4. Is immortality to be sought for? Romans 2:7. Is eternal life a FREE GIFT bestowed on those who seek for immortality? Same verse and Romans 6:23.

5. Now turn to 1 Corinthians 15:53 and 54. Do these two verses say that humans are immortal already? What must someone PUT ON? When will humans be clothed with immortality? Verse 52. Is this the time of the resurrection? 1 Thessalonians 4:16.

6. Did David, King of Israel, ascend to heaven as an immortal soul when he died? Acts 2:29 and 34. Has any man, except Christ, ascended to heaven? John 3:13. Will David become immortal when raised from the dead at the resurrection? Jeremiah 30:9.

COMMENT: Some, at this point, will think of Enoch and Elijah and assume that they prove that man has an immortal soul. If you have not read the truth about Enoch and Elijah, see the article titled "Where are Enoch and Elijah?" at COGwriter.com. You will be astounded at the answer!

7. Did David prophesy of the resurrection of Christ? Acts 2:30-31. What was David's specific prophecy? Verses 27 and 31. Does not this prove that the resurrection was demonstrated by the fact that Christ's soul was not left in Hades (the grave)?

COMMENT: The resurrection of Christ involved the resurrection of His soul – his BODY – from the grave.

The Greek word "psuche", translated "soul" and "life" in the King James Version, has the same meaning as the Hebrew word "nephesh". It was the "psuche" or soul – the body of Christ after his lifeblood was spilled – that was buried. That is what was resurrected!

Why a Resurrection?

If people were an immortal soul in a material body – and if the death of the body releases the soul – then there would be no need for a resurrection to immortal life. Humans would merely CONTINUE living after death. But THE VERY FACT THAT THE BIBLE TEACHES THE RESURRECTION FROM THE DEAD IS POSITIVE PROOF THAT HUMANS HAVE NO IMMORTAL SOUL. Here is further proof from your Bible!

1. IF Christ had not risen from the dead, would our faith be all in vain? 1 Corinthians 15:14, KJV. Why? Verse 17. And what has happened to those who already are dead in their graves, if Christ is STILL dead? Verse 18. Have they PERISHED forever?

2. However, did Christ Himself warn that the unregenerate, or unrepentant, man is to perish? John 3:16 and Luke 13:3, 5. If man were an immortal soul, could he actually perish? – or would he still keep on living? Isn't it plain that the word "perish" means to CEASE LIVING?

3. Notice the example of Adam. Was he permitted to eat the fruit of the "tree of [eternal] life" after he sinned? Genesis 3:22-24, especially last part of verse 22.

4. Would Adam and Eve have naturally lived forever as immortal souls, or would eternal life have come as a consequence of partaking of something NOT INHERENT in themselves? Genesis 3:22.

5. How did the Devil deceive Eve? Genesis 3:4. Isn't this the same lie which is being preached today as the doctrine of the immortality of the soul – saying a person already has eternal life inherent within oneself? Then is the Devil actually the originator of this false doctrine?

COMMENT: The "tree of life" symbolized the way to eternal life of the Holy Spirit. If Adam had eaten – partaken of – the fruit of that tree, rather than of the forbidden tree, he would have received the Holy Spirit which is the very life of God.

Adam was created incomplete. He was created to need the Holy Spirit of God in order to live forever. Adam, however, had to choose whether or not he would accept the free gift of the Holy Spirit. He chose NOT to receive the Holy Spirit by disobeying God and was thereafter cut off from access to the tree of life! Here is yet another proof that no man has eternal life INHERENT within himself.

6. Job once asked the question, "If a man dies, shall he live again?" (Job 14:14.) What was Job's answer to his own question? Same verse.

7. Did Job speak of a CHANGE that was yet coming? What was that change? 1 Corinthians 15:51-53. When will it take place?

8. When that change comes, what will Job, David and all those in the resurrection be like? Psalm 17:15. Will we be like God in the resurrection? Is God spirit? Are we to be composed of spirit then? 1 Corinthians 15:44. Compare this with 1 John 3:2-3. Are we to be like Christ? Is Christ now composed of spirit? 2 Corinthians 3:17.

9. At the resurrection, who will HEAR the voice of the Son of God? John 5:25. Are immortal souls going to hear it, or are the DEAD going to hear?

COMMENT: The dead cannot hear unless there is a RESURRECTION! The dead are pictured as being ASLEEP IN THEIR GRAVES, awaiting the day of the resurrection. Notice Jesus' words when describing the death of Lazarus, the brother of Mary and Martha: "OUR FRIEND LAZARUS SLEEPS, but I go that I may WAKE HIM UP." Then His disciples said, "Lord, if he sleeps he will get well." However, JESUS SPOKE OF HIS DEATH, but they thought that He was speaking about taking rest in sleep. 14 Then Jesus said to them plainly, "Lazarus is dead (John 11:11-14).

Death is described as a sleep because THE DEAD ARE NOT CONSCIOUS. Notice the plain evidence of Scripture: "And many of those who SLEEP IN THE DUST of the earth shall awake" (Daniel 12:2). "and the graves were opened; and many bodies of THE SAINTS WHO HAD FALLEN ASLEEP were raised" (Matthew

27:52). "And when thy days be fulfilled," said God to David, "and thou shalt SLEEP with thy fathers ..." (2 Samuel 7:12, KJV).

DEATH IS described as a SLEEP over 36 times in the King James Version of the Bible when referring to the kings of Israel and Judah! "David SLEPT with his fathers" (1 Kings 2:10, KJV). Notice that it does not say "the body slept, but the soul was conscious." It plainly says, "DAVID slept." IT WAS THE CONSCIOUS PERSON WHO FELL ASLEEP IN DEATH!

In the following verses (KJV) the same expression is used to describe death. Look each one up and see for yourself that death is a sleep! 1 Kings 11:21, 43 and 14:20, 31 and 15:8, 24 and 16:6, 28 and 22:40, 50; 2 Kings 8:24 and 10:35 and 13:9, 13 and 14:16, 22, 29 and 15:7, 22, 38 and 16:20 and 20:21 and 21:18 and 24:6; 2 Chronicles 9:31 and 12:16 and 14:1 and 16:13 and 21:1 and 26:2, 23 and 27:9 and 28:27 and 32:33 and 33:20. You will find similar results in other translations.

CERTAINLY HERE IS EVIDENCE THAT THE DEAD ARE NOT CONSCIOUS. THE UNCONSCIOUS SPIRIT ESSENCE IN EACH MAN AND WOMAN – "THE SPIRIT IN MAN" – SLEEPS!

10. When the dead hear the voice of the Son of God at the resurrection, where will they come from – heaven? John 5:28-29. Or will they come out of their graves? If they come out of their graves, that is where they must have been! Notice that these verses do NOT say that the souls descend from heaven and join the bodies – rather the dead come to life through a resurrection and leave their graves to join Christ (1 Thessalonians 4:16-17).

11. When that INSTANTANEOUS CHANGE comes at the resurrection, are we to be clothed with - TO PUT ON - SPIRIT? 1 Corinthians 15:51-53 and 2 Corinthians 5:1-5, KJV. Is this spirit eternal? Last part of 2 Corinthians 5:1 and 2 Corinthians 4:18. Does the spirit which will compose us at the resurrection come down from heaven? Notice 2 Corinthians 5, verse 2. If we have been begotten of the Holy Spirit, after repenting, believing, and being baptized, do we even now have the "earnest" of the spirit? 2 Corinthians 5:5, KJV.

COMMENT: The "earnest" of the spirit means a small portion of spirit given by God to bind His bargain with us that He will finally give us eternal life. See a dictionary for the full definition of the word "earnest."

12. Unless we have the Holy Spirit abiding in us, have we any right to be called Christ's or Christians? Romans 8:9.

13. If the Holy Spirit dwells in us, will it be the agent by which God quickens, or makes alive, our mortal bodies at the resurrection? Romans 8:11. If we are begotten and led by the Spirit of God, what are we? Verse 14-15.

When Did Paul Expect to Be with Christ?

There are some who believe that when Christians die they go immediately to heaven to be with Christ. They claim Paul's statement in Philippians 1:23-24 as supposed proof. Let us study these verses, to see if they overthrow all the rest of Scripture and teach that man is an immortal soul after all.

1. Did Paul have a desire to be with Christ? Philippians 1:23. Should all Christians have the same desire?

2. But does this verse state WHERE Paul would go and WHEN he would be with Christ? No! There is not one word here mentioning heaven as the place Paul wanted to be, nor is there one word saying that Paul would be with Christ IMMEDIATELY. People read these ideas into the Bible, but they are not there!

3. Did Paul expect to be with Christ after he was "offered" – KILLED? 2 Timothy 4:6-8, KJV. Was the time of Paul's DEATH then at hand? What did he expect to receive from Christ when he would meet Him? Verse 8. When did he expect to receive this crown? What "day" is Paul referring to? – the day immediately after his death, or the day of the resurrection? Last part of verse 8. Isn't the time of Christ's appearing plainly the time of the resurrection?

4. When Christ returns, will He bring His rewards with Him to give to those who are resurrected? Isaiah 40:10 and Revelation 22:12.

5. When are all the Christians to meet the Lord? 1 Thessalonians 4:16-17.

COMMENT: Those who are dead in their graves are not conscious; they have no knowledge of passing time. The very next moment in their consciousnesses will be the time of the resurrection! That is why Paul wrote in 2 Corinthians 5:9-10: "Therefore we make it our aim, whether present [alive in the flesh] or absent [dead in the grave], to be well pleasing to Him"

When?

Verse 10 tells! At the judgment when Christ returns. That is when Paul expects to receive the reward of his labors! See 2 Timothy 4:1. Proof of a conscious immortal soul? No! Proof, rather, of the RESURRECTION, and of the "spirit in man" which sleeps until the resurrection.

Many people who believe that they will go to heaven when they die, consider the 2nd century philosopher Justin Martyr a saint. He wrote:

> For if you have fallen in with some who are called Christians, but ... who say there is no resurrection of the dead, and that their souls, when they die, are taken to heaven; do not imagine that they are Christians" (Dialogue. Chapter 80).

Also in the 2nd century, Church of God leader, Polycarp of Smyrna stated:

> I bless you for because you have considered me worthy of this day and hour, that I might receive a place among the number of martyrs in the cup of your Christ, to the resurrection to eternal life, both of soul and of body, in the incorruptibility of the Holy Spirit (The Martyrdom of Polycarp, 14:2).

The idea that Christians do not go to heaven upon death, but that there would be a physical resurrection, is not a new one.

Can the Soul Be Destroyed?

Another scripture is frequently quoted in an attempt to support the ERRONEOUS doctrine of the immortality of the soul. That scripture is Matthew 10:28. Open your Bible to this verse and read it.

1. According to Matthew 10:28, is the soul something that can be DESTROYED? Then doesn't Jesus plainly show that the "SOUL" IS NOT IMMORTAL? Let's understand exactly what Jesus is talking about.

2. Aren't Christians to reckon themselves as already being SYMBOLICALLY DEAD through water baptism? Romans 6:4 and 11.

3. Is the "old man" – the OLD SINFUL LIFE OR SOUL – TO HAVE BEEN CRUCIFIED with Christ? Romans 6:3-6. Is this old carnal mind, the CARNAL ATTITUDE, the carnal self or soul, to be reckoned as figuratively having DIED with Christ? Verse 8.

COMMENT: When a person repents of their sins, God requires that individual to FIGURATIVELY KILL one's own old sinful soul, or life, by being immersed, or baptized – BURIED – in water.

4. Since CHRISTIANS HAVE ALREADY RECKONED THEIR SINFUL LIVES – OR THEIR SOULS – AS DEAD with Christ, is the body the only remaining thing which men can kill? Matthew 10:28. Let's understand the full significance of this scripture.

COMMENT: Men can kill the body, but not the truth of the resurrection.

Humans can kill our bodies, but they can do no more. Christians have already reckoned our lives dead upon baptism. The new life we now live is by the faith of Jesus Christ in us. "For ye are dead, and your life is hid with Christ in God" (Col. 3:3). Jesus brings out the great importance of the fact that the first or natural life (soul) of a Christian is already perished. There is nothing of that life which remains for men to kill.

That is why Jesus declared that man can kill the body, but not the soul or life. We are figuratively dead already — our physical way of life is crucified. But the life of Christ in us can't be touched by man; he cannot kill it because it is Christ's very own life. Although the original word for "eternal life" is from another Greek word, Jesus uses psuche — soul or material life — because Christ is living His life in our material bodies.

Notice how:

> The mind of a new convert is begotten at conversion by the Spirit of God. A NEW SPIRITUAL life actually begins! But the Spirit of God is NOT ANOTHER CONSCIOUSNESS; it is spiritual life from God that joins with the human spirit IN the man and converts the conscious mind into a "new creature" — or CREATION — with the potential of eternal life.

Most people do not understand the meaning of the word "conversion." It is a CHEMICAL term. It means "to change the nature of." In other words, the Spirit of God, which is added to your mind when you repent and surrender your life to Him, IS THE AGENT BY WHICH YOUR CARNAL MIND IS TO BE CHANGED INTO A SPIRITUAL MIND — CHANGED from a being of corruptible flesh with a carnal mind INTO A SPIRITUAL BEING — ACTUALLY COMPOSED OF SPIRIT, with the power of an endless life! Conversion, then, ultimately means much more than a change of attitude. It includes a change in composition — A CHANGE FROM PHYSICAL MATTER TO IMMORTAL SPIRIT!

But this change does not take place all at once. It BEGINS WHEN YOU BECOME BEGOTTEN by the Spirit of God. In this life what is changed is your attitude, your character, your mind's outlook on life. It is NOT UNTIL THE RESURRECTION THAT YOU ARE TO BE COMPLETELY CONVERTED into spirit. It is at the resurrection that this conversion is finally completed! At death your conscious self dies. Your mind ceases to think (Ecclesiastes 9:5). But the power or Spirit of God that begot the new spiritual life within you is reserved in heaven and will recreate your mind and your character from the MOLD of your human spirit which has been asleep. For those still alive at the moment of Christ's return, the power of God will quicken or make immortal their mortal bodies. That new spiritual life now begotten within you — if you have truly been begotten by God — even though it LOSES CONSCIOUSNESS AT DEATH, your enemies have no power over. It is your RIGHT to eternal life which no MAN can take from you!

But IF YOU WILLFULLY REBEL against God and become incorrigible after the knowledge of the truth is manifest to your mind, GOD WILL DESTROY BOTH THE BODY AND ANY CHANCE OF A FUTURE LIFE ("SOUL") IN GEHENNA-FIRE! You will be burned up! And from that there will never be a resurrection. That will be your end for all eternity! But more about this in the next lesson.

"Body, Soul and Spirit"?

The pagan philosophers believed that man was an immortal soul in a material body. The Catholic Church has ADOPTED this view.

Furthermore, many PROTESTANTS today CLAIM THAT MAN IS "BODY, SOUL AND SPIRIT." But as to which is immortal — the soul or the spirit — they never seem quite sure! Now let us notice what THE BIBLE REVEALS about "body, soul and spirit."

1. Does not the apostle Paul sometimes refer to man as "body, soul, and spirit"? 1 Thessalonians 5:23. Does this verse prove the doctrine of the "immortality of the soul"? What does the word "spirit" mean in 1 Thessalonians 5:23? Turn to 1 Corinthians 2:11 for the answer. It refers to the human spirit essence IN mortal man.

2. Isn't it rather plain that Paul, in 1 Thessalonians 5:23, is referring to the POWER OF MIND when he uses the word "SPIRIT"? And to the physical LIFE when he uses the word "SOUL"? And to the FLESH when he uses the word "BODY"? WHAT'S WRONG WITH HAVING YOUR WHOLE MIND, your LIFE, and your BODY PRESERVED BLAMELESS — PRESERVED FROM THE PENALTY OF SIN — in anticipation of the coming of Christ? Compare 2 Corinthians 7:1 with 1 Thessalonians 5:23.

COMMENT: How plain the Bible is. Humans are MORTAL, corruptible flesh — organic matter with a temporary life. Humans have NO immortal soul. Humans have no hope of a future life, except for the intervention of the Almighty. And God did intervene to send His Son to make possible through the Gospel a new birth — a new life as Spirit — and immortality. Because all have sinned — because the human race has made itself utterly miserable, God commands people everywhere to REPENT, to believe in Jesus Christ, to be baptized and to receive the Holy Spirit. God has given this plan because He loves us — because he has "no pleasure in the death of the wicked, ... TURN, TURN from your evil ways! FOR WHY should you DIE," asks the Almighty in Ezekiel 33:11.

God wants repentance and will bestow eternal life to Christians in the first resurrection (1 Corinthians 15:50-54).

1. WHERE DOES THE LIFE OF ALL LIVING CREATURES RESIDE? Genesis 9:4. Is the life of man and animals found in the BLOODSTREAM? – or in an immortal soul?

2. Do we find the same definition of life in Leviticus 17:11 and 14?

3. Does Deuteronomy 12:23 corroborate this?

COMMENT: In these verses, the Hebrew word NEPHESH is translated "life." The word NEPHESH or soul, then, can mean either the FLESHLY PART of a person or the LIFEBLOOD of a person.

4. Did Christ make His soul an offering for sin? Isaiah 53:10. How did He accomplish this? Verse 12.

COMMENT: Christ gave Himself for our sins (1 Corinthians 15:3) – offered up His soul or body to be crucified, and allowed His lifeblood or soul to be poured out!

5. When a person dies – becomes lifeless – what happens to him? Ecclesiastes 9:5. How much do the dead know?

COMMENT: Since the dead are not conscious of anything, then a human is NOT born with an immortal soul which would be aware of things happening around it after man's fleshly body dies.

6. Are those who have died able to praise God? Psalm 115:17. Does this sound like what most of you have been taught in the churches? Do the churches really believe and teach the Bible?

7. Is there any remembrance of God in death? Psalm 6:5.

COMMENT: DEATH is the OPPOSITE OF LIFE. Death is the CESSATION OF LIFE.

Is a HuMan Merely an Animal?

1. Since both humans and animals maintain their mortal existence by the very same breath – is a human MERELY AN ANIMAL? Isn't man created in the image of God? Genesis 1:26-27. Are humans to rule over all other creatures? Verse 26.

2. Were animals created in God's image or weren't they created each after its own kind? Genesis 1:21, 24, 25.

3. Other than the "spirit in man," what is it that makes humans different from the animals – the lower creatures of the earth that God created? Was a human to be made in the image and likeness of God? Did God, then, create a mortal being – a human – after His own kind – the God kind? Genesis 1:26-27.

COMMENT: The Hebrew words of Genesis 1:26-27 reveal God's great plan and ultimate purpose for humankind! When God moulded Adam of the dust, Adam was shaped in the "likeness" – the outward form and shape – of God Himself! God didn't form any of the other creatures He had created to be a clay replica of Himself.

Notice what else God gave humans at creation! "God said, Let Us make man in OUR IMAGE ... " The Hebrew words here indicate more than merely the outward form and shape of God – His likeness – FAR MORE! The image of God refers to aspects of His MIND AND CHARACTER! No animal was ever given the gift of mind power! It is this very special attribute of mind and character that separates humans from animals!

A human IS NOT A MERE ANIMAL! Animals have only the brain – fantastically intricate brain with a degree of memory and instinct – which God created for each kind of animal. BUT ANIMALS DO NOT HAVE THE POTENTIAL OF MIND AND CHARACTER GOD CREATED ONLY FOR HUMANS.

Notice the great difference. Animals have brains as well as humans. Yet animals DO NOT HAVE TRUE REASONING, THINKING MINDS!

Animals follow habit patterns in their feeding, nesting, migration, and reproduction – by INSTINCT. This instinct which God created in their brains is set like a clock to cause them to react INVOLUNTARILY.

For example, thousands of birds flock south as winter approaches in the northern hemisphere each year without KNOWING WHY, without planning ahead an itinerary of stops. Yet at a given signal – like the alarm of a clock – they leave their summer feeding grounds in the North and travel thousands of miles south. Scientists don't fully understand WHY – they can merely observe the operation of this animal instinct which God created. Each species of bird – each kind God created – has different instinctive patterns, builds different nests, feeds on different foods, and migrates in different ways at different times to different places. None of these actions are planned by animals however; they are merely the reaction Almighty God built into the instinct of each creature at creation.

But a HUMAN is DIFFERENT! A human is able to see – to perceive and understand – various ways to do any one thing. Humans can reason from memorized facts and knowledge, draw conclusions, make decisions, will to act according to a thought-out plan. Animals have much, much, less reasoning abilities.

Each person may build a different house, eat different foods – live an entirely different way of life from every other. If a human wants to change a particular way of life, this can be done! Human beings are not subject to the type of instinct, governed by a set of pre-determined natural principles, as are animals.

Humans can CHOOSE – HUMANS HAVE FREE MORAL AGENCY! Humans can devise codes of morals and exercise self-discipline. Humans can originate ideas and evaluate scientific knowledge because humans have MINDS which were made in the "image" of God's own mind! Humans can devise, plan, and bring those plans to fruition – because humans have some of the same creative powers God Himself has! BUT PEOPLE'S POWERS ARE LIMITED NOW (cf. Hebrews 2:8)!

The attributes of mind and character make humans God's unique physical creation. God has shared some of His own qualities – the image of His mind – with humans – and expects humans to love and to develop the IMAGE of GOD'S PERFECT HOLY CHARACTER.
That is the wonderful purpose God is working out here below! God gave humans the ability to choose right from wrong – and commands people to choose RIGHT! By constantly choosing God's ways – making the right decisions God Himself would make, a human can develop the very character image of Almighty God!

This is what a human was designed to become at creation. This is the wonderful reason why humans were made different from animals, and given – IN A LIMITED WAY – some of the very attributes of God!
God's plan is to make of humans – now only a CLAY model of the God kind – partakers of God's Own Divine Nature! God is reproducing himself IN HUMANKIND– and converted humans will someday be elevated to the God KIND!

To understand more of God's wonderful purpose for humankind, you should read "What is the Meaning of Life?" available at COGwriter.com. The purpose for human life is the heart and core of Christ's Gospel. No wonder those who couldn't understand His message accused Him of BLASPHEMY!

More FREE *Continuing Church of God* Books and Booklets
at www.ccog.org/books

Proof Jesus is the Messiah

The Decalogue, Christianity, and the Beast

Should You Keep God's Holy Days or Demonic Holidays?

Where Is The True Christian Church Today?

Youth & Singles: Q&A

By Bob Thiel

The following are from our free online booklet, *Dating: A Key to Success in Marriage*, a practical dating guide for Christians.

This first question was the one the old Worldwide Church of God said it got from teens more often than any other.

Q. I am crazy about this really cute guy (or gal), but he (she) doesn't seem to know I exist. How can I get him (her) to notice me and like me?

A. The answer is that you can't. That's right, you can't get someone of the opposite sex to like you.
Don't misunderstand. This doesn't mean you are helpless to find friends of the opposite sex, or that you are doomed to a life of loneliness. There is much you can and should do if you want to have friends (Proverbs 18:24) and someday find an appropriate spouse.

In time, the person you have interest in may end up being interested in you. But you cannot force that.

You might be able to get them to notice you, but depending on them and what you do, you may turn them away from you instead of towards you.

It's not a matter of what you can get. It's a matter of what you can give.

If you are a giver, other givers will tend to be attracted to you (as will takers—so be cautious about prematurely settling for someone just because they may pay attention to you).

Q. Is it okay to wear more revealing clothes or buy an impressive car to get someone's romantic interest?

A. No.

Even if you can get someone's attention by your appearance, the car you may drive, money, smooth conversational skills, etc. that will not make them like you or truly love you.

Do you really want to marry someone that you have impressed by making yourself look seductive or by the car you drive?

If you flaunt your body or your money, eventually the one you attract is likely to leave for one who flaunts 'better' than you.

Consider also that the Bible teaches:

> 22 Flee also youthful lusts; but pursue righteousness, faith, love, peace with those who call on the Lord out of a pure heart. (2 Timothy 2:22)

Christians are to have a pure heart and not pursue youthful lusts.

Those who are mainly attracted by lusts of the flesh tend to let their lusts control them and are not likely to stay with you. Those with wandering eyes, tend to continue to wander.

A Christian man does not want an immoral lust provoking seductress as his wife.

Teens and singles (as well as married people) should dress appropriately (cf. 1 Timothy 2:9-10).

We are open to covering other questions that are not in our booklet as well. If you have appropriate questions that you would like answered here, you can send them to the Continuing Church of God at the address shown in the front of this magazine or send an email for consideration.

Made in the USA
Middletown, DE
22 December 2018